Networking Like a Pro!

20 Tips On Turning the Contacts You Get Into the Connections You Need

Brian Hilliard

James Palmer

Agito Consulting

Atlanta

1st Printing   ISBN 0-9743711-0-6

I would like to dedicate this book to all the people who helped me make it a reality.

To Trisha Alcock, for her vision and tireless effort throughout the entire process. To Amy Windham, whose countless thoughts and recommendations provided the fuel for making this work. To Dr. Sean McWilliams, who was with us from the very beginning. And finally, to co-author James Palmer and Chris Redwood, whose dedication and expertise helped keep everything on track.

Thank you all.

Introduction

Imagine confidently creating contacts with everyone you meet. Sound too good to be true? We don't think so.

Networking Like a Pro! is for job seekers looking to land that next big assignment, and business people looking to win their next deal. If you're new to the world of networking, or even a seasoned pro, you'll walk away with practical techniques you can use right away.

This book goes beyond just "working the room," and focuses on the one question that should be at the top of everyone's list: How can I differentiate myself in the minds of other people from everyone else they've met?

And if we know that networking is less about meeting new people than it is having them remember you after the fact, then using our proven techniques is a must for any networking professional.

We've divided this book into two sections, with the first half focusing on creating a "visible identity." These tips range from "Three Surefire Ways for Starting a Conversation" to "Becoming a Better Listener with One Simple Technique."

The second half focuses on accelerating your success after the event is over. We discuss how long to wait when following up with a person you've just met, and what to say during that conversation.

Each of our tips is a simple, yet powerful tool that represents the collective wisdom of other networking professionals, as well as our own experience. You'll also notice that while each tip is a "free-standing" technique, collectively they create a solid foundation to be used in any networking situation.

So take a look at the many examples, both here and on our Web site, and then start Networking Like a Pro!

20

Create a Visible Identity

Three Surefire Ways for Starting a Conversation

One of the toughest things for most people is to meet and talk to someone whom they've never met before. Whether you're at a networking event or going out on a blind date, starting a conversation with someone you don't know is never easy.

But rest assured, when it comes to networking at least, you'll always have one thing on your side: Everyone else in the room is looking to do the exact same thing. In other words, they all want to meet and talk to other business professionals.

With that in mind, you really do not need any witty remarks or "show stopping" one-liners to get people's attention. All you need to do is find a topic or two that gets the conversation started, and go from there.

Here are a few "primers" that I like to use to get started.

The Weather

Okay, this probably won't be the flashiest conversation starter you'll ever use, but you'd be surprised at how effective it is at breaking the ice. A comment that I'll use during evening networking events goes like this:

"Gorgeous day today, huh? Did you get a chance to go out and enjoy it a little?"

This question is perfect for situations when you're already in the general area of another individual, but you just haven't started a conversation yet. Examples of that could be standing in line at the registration table, or as you're getting a bite to eat.

> Making a quick comment about the speaker during that initial networking session is a real underrated way to drum up conversation.

Traffic

Here's another good standby, especially if you live in Atlanta, where rush hour traffic always seems to be a topic of conversation. Again, don't get too fancy here because all we're trying to do is get the ball rolling. As an example, I'd recommend something like this:

"Boy, I heard traffic was a killer getting down here. Were you able to make it over all right?"

From there the person will either tell you yes they did or no they didn't, but either way, both of you are talking.

A comment/thought about the speaker

Most of the networking events I've attended usually follow the same format. They schedule the first thirty minutes or so for event registration and initial networking. Then comes a speaker who spends another half hour on a topic of group interest (networking, effective communication, etc). And from there, the evening is usually capped off with some additional time to meet folks who you might have missed earlier.

Assuming this sequence holds true for your event, a comment about the speaker during that initial networking session is a real underrated way to drum up conversation.

"So, have you had a chance to hear [speaker's name] speak before? I understand she's a real expert on [topic]."

Needless to say, this works best if you've actually heard the person speak before, because then you can add to the conversation by giving your impressions of the previous event. If not though, that's fine. All you have to do is say you haven't heard her talk either, but you're really looking forward to getting her thoughts on this particular topic.

For those of you who are not naturally outgoing people, starting a conversation is never going to be an easy proposition. But if you keep in mind that everyone is looking to meet new people and that, generally speaking, there is no "bad" conversation starter, then you'll be well on your way to networking like a pro.

Become a Better Listener with One Simple Technique

Have you ever wondered why most people are better speakers than listeners? Or noticed when you were talking to someone, you can tell by their response that they were only "half listening" to what you were saying?

Well if you, or someone you know, is looking to become a more effective networker, then Focused Attention is a great listening technique to help you achieve that goal.

Let's say you're at a networking event, and you're listening to a really fast talker, somewhere in the neighborhood of 150 words per minute. And while that person is talking, let's say your brain is thinking at a rate of 400 words per minute.

So if you're thinking at a rate of 400 words per minute, and the person you're talking to is speaking at a rate of 150 words per minute, then what you do with that "extra" capacity (400 words minus 150 words per minute) is going to determine how good a listener you are.

Focused attention says to concentrate 100 percent of your attention on the message that the other person is giving.

Where is your attention focused? Are you planning your response while the other person is talking,

Fact: The human brain, on average, can think at a rate of 400 to 450 words per minute; the average person, however, can only talk at a rate of 100 to 150 words per minute.

or are you understanding their point and making a few mental notes to help you process it? Are you scanning the room to find the next person you want to meet, or if someone walks over, do you stop and devote your full attention to this person?

The reason most people aren't very good listeners is because during most discussions, they're spending their "extra" intellectual capacity (those extra 250 words we were just talking about) on everything other than the conversation at hand.

And in today's email-typing, pager-answering, voicemail-checking world where "multi-tasking" is very much en vogue, everyone seems to be doing two or three things at once.

Recommendation: At your next networking event, make it a point to "block out" everyone else in the room and focus your mental attention on what this person is saying.

A friend of mine once told me that he met somebody who went a step further than that: Whenever someone walked into his office, he physically removed whatever documents he was working on from his desk, and redirected his attention to that person. Wow! Now that sends a powerful message.

Imagine if you could send that same message to someone else in your life. It could be your spouse talking about their day at the dinner table, or a person at work trying to get your opinion on an important project they're working on.

Concentrating 100 percent of your attention on that person is a surefire way to make them feel their message is valued. And at the end of the day, isn't that what being a good listener is all about?

Three Easy Questions to Stand Out from the Crowd

Question: Generally speaking, during most conversations, do people like to talk more about themselves, or other people?

Answer: Themselves.

Question: Generally speaking, during most conversations, do people tend to talk more than they listen, or listen more than they talk?

Answer: Talk more than they listen.

Extra credit: At networking events, if you're listening while they're talking, and then you ask a good follow-up question based on the information you just heard, you're going to be more or less likely to stand out in their minds?

Answer: More likely.

And if you know that networking is less about meeting new people than it is having them remember you after the fact, then asking the right questions is a vital step in standing out from the crowd.

So how do you get someone to remember you from the other people he met that very same night?

Well, one technique we talked about earlier is a term called "Focused Attention" (Tip #2), and it's one of my favorites when it comes to effective listening skills.

Another good way to stand out is to ask the "right" questions during your conversation. What are some examples of these questions you ask? Let's take a look at a few of my favorites:

So where else do you normally network?

Amy Windham, a sales and marketing colleague of mine here in Atlanta, first brought this one to my attention and it's an absolute gem. Not only does this help break the ice during that sometimes awkward period just after you've introduced yourself, but it also gives you a chance to talk about something you both know a little bit about.

> ...this helps break the ice during that sometimes awkward period just after you've introduced yourself...

Another reason I like this question is because it gives you the opportunity to make an "instant connection" with that other person.

How? By providing valuable information they might not have had before. And as we all know, one of the keys to creating a solid business contact is to make a connection with that individual.

As an example, I was at a networking event one morning when I asked the gentleman I was speaking with where else he normally networked. He told me that as a matter of fact, he didn't know of too many other places around town because he just moved to the area.

Well that was music to my ears, because as someone who's lived in Atlanta for almost five years, I like to consider myself somewhat of an expert when it comes to local networking events. So I gave him the names of a couple of groups off the top of my head, and I mentioned that I would shoot him an email when I thought of some more.

You could almost see the relief in his eyes. He was genuinely grateful that I was helping him out with that information.

And that's what I mean when I talk about creating a connection with someone, and developing a solid business contact. If that were you, would you remember me after that event?

You bet!

What do you like best about what you do?

This is another good question I like to ask early in the conversation because, in my opinion, it's a little "fresher" than the old approach, "So what do you do?" Everyone's been asked that one before, and the new question gives you another option for getting that same information.

One caveat though: About 40 percent of the time I ask this question, people turn it right around and ask me the same thing. So don't say I didn't warn you!

Oh I see. What got you started in that direction?

This is a great question to ask during the latter stages of the conversation, and of the three questions we've talked about, this usually will elicit the longest response.

And that's okay, because now we're getting ready to wind down our conversation, while at the same time learning a little bit about what motivates this person.
As an example, you could have a conversation that sounds like this:

"Oh I see, you're in the sales and marketing field. What got you started in that direction?"

And off you go, finishing up a good, meaningful dialogue. Try these questions out at your next networking event;
I think you'll be pleasantly surprised.

If you have some favorites you've either used or have heard someone else use, please contact me at bhilliard@agitoconsulting.com. I'd be happy to add them to my list.

TIP 4

Change your Perspective...and What you Talk About

"What About Me?" is a fundamental principle when it comes to effective networking, and it says to put yourself in the other person's shoes, and then ask yourself what it is you would want to get out of that interaction. In other words, "What About Me?" requires you to change your perspective from yourself to the other person.

What is it she wants to hear? In a networking situation, you have a couple of options when it comes to the type of information you provide to others. A basic exchange means giving the same type of information people have heard over and over again. An example of this would be your name, your background, and perhaps what industry you're looking to get back into if you're currently seeking employment.

A basic exchange isn't all that bad, because how else would you get to know people if you didn't have some inkling of who they are and what they're all about? But where most people make their mistake is by continuing to go down this path by asking the same old questions (and hearing the same old responses) of everyone they meet.

"So what do you do?" is a perfect example of a question I've heard at least a thousand times. It's not a bad question per se, but there are better alternatives to help you stand out from the crowd. (For a healthy alternative to this question, please see Tip #3.)

The second option, in terms of providing information to someone, is to differentiate yourself by creating a meaningful dialogue with this person. How do you do that? Let's take a look at a few examples, keeping the "What About Me?" tool in mind.

Become a resource

Examples of this could be a report you saw on television, an article you read in the newspaper, something your spouse mentioned at breakfast, or a conversation you overheard at lunch. It doesn't make a difference where you got the information, as long as it's relevant to the person you're talking to.

> It doesn't make a difference where you got the information, as long as it's relevant to the person you're talking to.

As an example, let's say you're going to a networking function in which there will be a number of job seekers in attendance. Something they may be interested in is a job lead you found which didn't fit your skill set exactly, but based on your conversation with this person right now, might be something he should follow up on.

If job leads aren't something you're running into much lately, then another type of pertinent information could be this:

"You know, I saw a report the other day saying Atlanta was two months ahead of the rest of the country for coming out of this recession. I've noticed a little bit of that myself, but is this something you've seen?"

In this example, you've provided some information he may not have known, and you've asked for some input to keep the conversation going. How different will that conversation be from the ones he's had with everyone else? My guess is a lot.

For additional information on how you can gain access to the type of information that can make you a resource, please see "Top 5 Reasons Why You Should Read Every Day" (Tip #6).

Become a matchmaker

Another way to have a meaningful dialogue with people is to link that individual to someone else in your professional network who could be of service to him.

Going back to that job-seeking event from our previous example, a great way to accomplish this is to introduce him to a hiring manager who may be filling a position outside your industry. If you don't know of anyone who fits that bill, then what about an introduction to a person who isn't necessarily a hiring manager, but is plugged into that industry?

Who knows how that meeting will end up? Your contact just might know someone who could help the person you're talking to right now. But even if your introduction doesn't hit a "home run" like that, you've still gone a long way towards allowing yourself to stand out in that other person's mind.

And at the end of the day, isn't that what it's all about?

Expand your Network! Engage the Keynote Speaker

What is the biggest networking opportunity most people miss when attending an event? For me, the answer is as plain as day. Most people forget to include the speaker on their list of people with whom they should network. I'm not sure why this happens, but I think it's because most people think the speaker is either too busy, or doesn't want to be bothered with what they have to say.

Whatever your reasoning may be, I strongly recommend getting past any nagging doubts, and start networking with people who make their living by talking in front of groups. As a motivational speaker, I thoroughly enjoy talking to audience members before, during, and after an event at which I've spoken.

In fact, a majority of speakers I know put so much time and effort into their material, that a big part of the "payoff" is getting positive feedback from folks who've enjoyed the show. And from the perspective of the attendee, what better way to generate new potential contacts, than to plug yourself into the network of someone who spends a large amount of time talking to groups with interests similar to your own?

So with that in mind, let's take a look at how you can best engage the speaker before, during, and after their presentation.

Make small talk before the event.

This technique works best if you've done a little research on the person beforehand, or have an idea of what he's going to talk about.

As an example, you might say something like this:

"Hi Dan, my name is Brian Hilliard and I understand you'll be speaking today about [Topic]. Can you give me a quick preview on what you're going to cover?"

Now, that wasn't so bad, was it? You introduced yourself, got the conversation started, and bang! You're having a regular networking discussion, just like you would have with anyone else.

Recommendation: When you're registering for your next networking event, ask someone at the desk to point out the speaker (assuming you haven't seen him before) and then walk over and engage him in conversation.

Ask a (good) question during the presentation.

Most often, good speakers provide the audience with a chance to ask them questions, and this is a great opportunity to get yourself noticed by that individual. However, if you're going to do that, listening and preparation is key, since the last thing you want to do is start a discussion on a point that was already covered.

> ...good speakers provide the audience with a chance to ask them questions, and this is a great opportunity to get yourself noticed...

Oh, and one more thing. If at all possible, try to ask a question or make a point that somehow goes along with a previous point the speaker made. It's not bad to disagree, but remember, your objective is to get yourself noticed by this person in a positive light (at least from his perspective), and a good way to do that is to be "in line" with where he wants to go. So if you're thinking about playing devil's advocate during the middle of the session, just keep in mind that this might not be the best way to get that person into your corner.

Initiating a follow-up discussion after the presentation.

If you're an entrepreneur or sales professional, engaging the speaker after the event is a great way to "go straight to the top," without having all the red tape normally associated with the process. After all, if this person wasn't relatively high up in the organization, then he probably wouldn't be talking to your group in the first place. So why not engage a potential decision maker with something like this:

"Dan, Brian Hilliard. [Shake hands.] As someone who's spoken in front of groups myself, I can honestly say that you did a great job up there. [Pause.] Hey listen, during your presentation you mentioned that your company was increasing its online presence through a renewed Web site design and marketing initiative...how have you partnered with other organizations in achieving those goals?"

Now that's a question! And I can guarantee he probably hasn't heard that one before. So now he'll tell you what a great question that is, and he'll give you a little more information on where he was going with that point. And, if we make the assumption that your company happens to be in the field of Web site design and marketing, then all you do is ask for his card, and see if you can touch base with him at a later date.

And there you have it, instant contact.

There's one more thing to remember when engaging speakers after the event: Try to keep your comments relatively short. Not only is the person physically spent from being on stage for the last 45 minutes (remember, he's been standing that whole time), but others are probably waiting to talk to him as well.

So, just follow the previous script, tailor it to your particular service offering, and you'll be out of there in under a minute.

Top Five Reasons Why You Should Read Every Day

One of the biggest ironies of the Information Age, is the large amount of data available for people who don't perceive themselves as having enough time to take it all in.

I remember 10 years ago, doing research usually meant a trip to the local library and matching wits with the Dewy Decimal System, only to find out what you needed wasn't there. Today, of course, things are much different. The problem isn't trying to get enough information; it's dealing with the overabundance of information on a daily basis. People are overwhelmed by the sheer volume of what's available.

While that's something I understand, it still doesn't change the fact that there's a wealth of business information out there that every professional should periodically access. So much so, that I've put together a list detailing the value of reading a business magazine or newspaper every day.

You may wonder, "What's so important about doing that every day?" Take a look at my Top 5 reasons, and you'll soon find out.

Helps keep you "in the loop," especially if you're a job seeker.

Let's face it, it's tough out there. The environment is changing and companies are doing more with less. If you're currently between jobs, it can feel like the business world is pass-

> ...when you read, you stay on top of the latest business news, while keeping your eyes open to what's going on in the industry.

ing you by. But, if you're looking to keep your professional "edge" while riding out these tough economic times, then reading an online magazine or newspaper is a great first step.

Why? Because when you read, you stay on top of the latest business news, while keeping your eyes open to what's going on in the industry. You're scouring the landscape to see what other companies are doing, while asking, "What new skills can I obtain to help me take advantage of these developing trends?"

Sound like a lot to ask from just one magazine? Well, it is. But try reading one magazine today, another tomorrow, and keep doing that for a week. I'd be surprised if you didn't see a noticeable "up tick" in your overall skill set.

And, with all of this good information out there, you're probably wondering where to start. Try accessing www.headlinespot.com. It has a number of links to city-specific magazine and newspaper Web sites. Check out the business section on the vertical menu bar on the left-hand side of the site, and take it from there.

Provides the material for "value added" information.

When you read everyday, you'll occasionally find an article that might be of interest to another business contact. When that happens, here's what you do: Cut out the article and stick a Post-it®, note on it. Jot down a quick message saying you thought this article might be of interest to them, and then mail it off. How easy is that?

The great thing about this technique is that you can use it with just about everyone you know. It could be a person you met last week, last month, or even last year. Time doesn't make too much of a difference, because the person wasn't expecting it in the first place. Your note will literally come out of the blue.

And what a great way to stay in touch with someone you haven't spoken with in awhile!

Helps you stand out during any networking event.

Earlier in the book, I talked about using information you pick up in magazines or trade journals to differentiate yourself from the crowd. I also mentioned how reading on a continual basis can help you become a "resource" in that other person's mind. To see some examples on how you can do this, please reference our "What About Me?" technique in Tip #4.

Stimulates new ideas, especially if you're an entrepreneur.

Reading business magazines is a great way to step back from the day-to-day nature of your business, and see things from a different angle. Sometimes it seems like you spend more time "fighting fires" than strategizing where you want your business to be in three years.

But, if you want to sharpen your long-term focus while keeping your short-term "edge," then consider reading a few articles every day and implementing those new ideas. And for you "bottom line" business people out there, I can attest to the fact that reading alone has added three to five percentage points to my company, with all of the good ideas it gave me.

> ...I can attest to the fact that reading alone has added three to five percentage points to my company, with all of the good ideas it gave me.

"Three to five percentage points?" you ask. "That sounds like a lot." Well, maybe so, but how do you think I thought about writing this book?

Find potential job opportunities.

This can be a bit of a long shot for those seeking employment opportunities or prospective customers, and by no means would I recommend it as your only prospecting tool. With that said, reading newspaper articles can work in the context of finding new business opportunities. (And no, I'm not talking about the classified section.)

> ...one of the most notable workshops resulting from this technique was with a Super Bowl contending football team a few years back.

As an example, my mom, who's also a motivational speaker, spent the first 20 years of her business securing speaking engagements based on stories she saw in the newspaper. She sees a story, clips it out, and goes to work. As a matter of fact, one of the most notable workshops resulting from this technique was with a Super Bowl contending football team a few years back.

I know what you're thinking, "A Super Bowl team! That'll never work for me. And besides, even if I did want to try it out, how would I start?" Well, here's how it works:

Let's say you're an entrepreneur reading a story about a company facing a challenge you can address. After clipping out the article and doing some online research, you've confirmed your initial thought: Your business can help. Next, look up the names that appear in the article, and see if you can find their mailing addresses. If you can't find that information, consider contacting the reporter to see if he can point you in the right direction.

Send those individuals a short letter explaining that you saw their story in the newspaper, and you think you could provide some assistance. You should also state that you'll follow up with a phone call in a few days to discuss this opportunity further. (For an example of what this letter could look like, visit the articles section on our Web site www.agitoconsulting.com.)

And let me tell you something, as someone who's seen this work on many occasions, I can't think of a more direct way of expanding your professional network, short of actually meeting these individuals yourself.

"But I don't have the time."

I know what you're thinking, "Okay Brian, I understand why I need to be reading, and you've convinced me; but the bottom line is I just don't have the time." I can understand that too. There's so much going on in the business world today that sometimes it's a wonder we can even get up in the morning.

So here are a few "bonus tips" on how you can create more time for yourself in an otherwise swamped day.

Just about everyone drinks coffee or something similar to it in the morning. Instead of downloading emails or listening to your voicemail messages while drinking your next cup, try using that time to read a few articles from your favorite business magazine.

For those of you feeling a little bit more aggressive, consider "scheduling" 30 minutes into your day just for reading. This works best for individuals who work from home, or who have flexibility in their schedules. For me, I usually wait until the end of the day to do my reading, and I've found it to be a great way to "unwind," while getting some important business work done. Just enter it on your calendar like you would any other meeting, and go from there.

Also consider picking up some audio books you can listen to in the car.

This one's a slam-dunk because other than your office, where else do you spend the majority of your time during the work-week? If you're not sure where to start in terms of the specific books to read, swing by our "What I'm Reading" section on www.agitoconsulting.com and you'll find a list of the books I've recently enjoyed.

Reading should be an important part of every business-person's day. And with so much information available at the drop of a hat, the real question is how can you best take advantage of it?

Getting Your Card to the Top of the Stack

Ahh...the business card. A staple in the lives of professionals all over the world. The business card represents the first tangible impression someone has of you, and to a certain degree, shapes the level of communication you're going to have with that person later down the road.

Yet with so much riding on such a small piece of paper, I'm continually amazed at the number of people who haven't mastered the basics of the process—starting with how the business card is designed and the way it looks, to how it's delivered and making sure you have plenty of cards on you.

Make no mistake, when you pull out your business card, one of two things can happen: Your card can reinforce the perception that you're a sharp, competent individual, or it can do the exact opposite by looking "homemade" and unprofessional. It's completely up to you which image your card conveys. So with that in mind, let's take a look at three areas surrounding business cards that can help you come off looking like a pro.

Make your card "user friendly."

Think of your business card as comprising two parts. The first is located on the front, and this is an area where you have 100 percent control over the look, feel and layout of the card. For job seekers, you can include your phone number, email address, and perhaps your expertise as it relates to a particular industry. Needless to say, the front of your card is what people see first, and it's a great way to visually differentiate yourself from the competition.

The second part of your business card is the back, and while it is technically "your card," this area actually is reserved for the person you're handing it to. In other words, it needs to be left blank so they can jot down notes about you or your company.

> I can't tell you how many times I have been to networking events where I felt like a turnstile, as people handed me their cards... and then moved on to the next person.

Now I know that last recommendation will come easier to some than it will others, since other schools of thought advocate the liberal use of both sides of the business card. And there's nothing wrong with that. But, if your card has your company name and contact information on the front, and your mission statement or ideal job qualifications on the back, then there's no room for the other person to jot down notes on what you're all about.

I was at an event the other day where a woman was telling the group "what a good lead" looks like for her, and if we could help out in this area, it would be extremely beneficial. While she was talking about her ideal lead, it triggered the name of someone I thought she should meet based on the information I was just given.

Do you know where I wrote that name down? You guessed it, on the back of her card. Now if her card had been cluttered with her mission statement and corporate history, would I have taken the time to pull out a separate sheet of paper? Maybe, maybe not. But as a successful business person, why take that chance?

Wait for the person to ask you for your business card.

That might seem obvious at first, but I can't tell you how many times I have been to networking events where I felt like a turnstile, as people handed me their cards, spoke for 30 sec-

> Your card can reinforce the perception that you're a sharp, competent individual, or it can do the exact opposite by looking "homemade" and unprofessional.

onds, and then moved on to the next person. Part of that phenomenon has to do with people trying to "work the room" and get as many business cards as possible.

Without getting into all the reasons why that probably isn't the best strategy, let me ask you this: How much can you really find out about that person during a 90-second "conversation," when halfway through, you're already thinking about meeting the next person?

By forcing yourself to wait until the other person asks you for your card, you're creating some discipline that actually allows you to have a thoughtful discussion. At the same time, you're almost playing a game with yourself to make sure what you say is actually of interest to them.

Because if you completely missed the mark, they probably won't ask for your card.

We discussed this a little earlier in our "What About Me?" technique (Tip #4), where you hit the points people want to hear. So what better way to "gauge" your networking success, than to see how many people ask for your card at the end of the conversation?

If the person doesn't ask, that's not a problem either. All you do is ask for theirs, and hand them yours in the process. Obviously that's not the ideal situation, but just because they didn't ask for your card doesn't necessarily mean you didn't do a good job of interacting with them.

Maybe they were on their way out the door, having a bad day, or simply thinking about something else. But if you're engaging, interesting, and adding value to the conversation, then more times than not, you should have no problem getting people to ask you for your card.

Make your cards look professional.

For individuals who currently are in transition or just starting up a business, Vista Print®, does a great job of printing professional-looking cards, and I understand they'll do it for a really good price. Do yourself a favor and order a set online. For those of you currently employed in a small business or entrepreneurial situation, you need to have your cards professionally printed. No ifs, ands, or buts about it.

As we said before, your business card represents the first tangible impression someone has of both you and the company you represent. So you don't want to pitch a $2,000 deal to a prospective client, while handing him a card that looks as if it was on the "buy one get one" shelf at the office supply store. Believe me, I've seen it happen before and it wasn't pretty.

If you need help finding a printer who can do it at a reasonable rate, give me a call and I'd be happy to point you in the right direction.

...what better way to "gauge" your networking success, than to see how many people ask for your card at the end of the conversation...

And with all of this talk about business cards, I don't need to remind you to keep some with you at all times. I'd recommend putting some in your car, purse, wallet, or anything you carry on a consistent basis.

Because you never know who you're going to meet when you're networking like a pro.

Increase Your Reach by Joining a Referral Group

For those of you who may be unfamiliar with this term, a referral group usually consists of 10 to 20 entrepreneurs, salespeople or small business owners from noncompeting industries, who meet once a week to "exchange leads."

As an example, let's say I meet someone at a networking event who's looking to create a marketing program for his small business. I know that isn't my forte, but I also know someone in my referral group who could do just that sort of thing. So, I'd take that person's contact information, give it to Amy Windham from my referral group, and she would follow up with a phone call to see if he's interested in learning how her services can help his business.

The best thing about the referral groups I've seen is that they "lock out" your competition by not allowing anyone else in your industry to join that particular group. So let's say you're in real estate, and someone else in the group runs into a person looking to buy a house. That person will be pointed in your direction, since no one else in the group is directly competing with you for that business.

In essence, by joining a referral group, you've effectively created a sales team that can help you plug into the networks of other people in your group. "Great deal," you're thinking. "So what's the catch?"

Well, there actually are two, but both are easy to overcome.

First, you have to be 100 percent committed to learning the businesses of every other group member, otherwise, how can you spot a good lead for them when you're networking? Second, you need to attend a majority of the weekly meetings, so you can stay abreast of the latest happenings and continue to pass out leads. If you fall short in either of these areas, chances are other group members will notice, and they'll be less inclined to pass leads your way because of their perception that you're not really looking out for them.

But, if your schedule allows you to attend these weekly meetings, and you're truly committed to finding leads for other members within your group, then joining a good referral group is a great way to increase your networking "reach."

Deliver Your Message with Confidence

Have you ever spoken with someone who's been job seeking for a while, and it looks like their heart just isn't in it anymore? You know, where once confident, optimistic people now appear anything but that.

What do you think happens to their job-hunting prospects when other people (read hiring managers) begin noticing a loss of confidence? The hiring manager feels less comfortable offering that person a position, and a vicious cycle begins: A loss of confidence leads to a lack of job offers, which leads to an even further loss of confidence.

So, what can you do to nip that in the bud, even after you've been out of work for quite some time? I have a few thoughts that can help you, or anyone else for that matter, get back on track.

Consider volunteering to help those who are less fortunate than you.

"Volunteer my time! While I'm trying to get a job?" That's exactly right. Volunteering to help those who are less fortunate is a great way for you to keep everything else in perspective.

Sure the economy is down, and yes you want a job that can keep you from worrying about your financial well-being, in

> What do you think happens to their job-hunting prospects when other people begin noticing a loss of confidence?

addition to that of your family. No question about it, these are both real concerns that every job seeker faces.

But when you compare it with some of the challenges other people face, such as debilitating medical conditions, homelessness and physical handicaps, you may be able to gain valuable insight into your own situation that you may not have seen before.

And when I talk about volunteering your time, I'm only suggesting four to five hours a month as a way to expose yourself to people who are in a different situation than you.

You'll be surprised what that can do for your self-confidence and the perception others have of you.

Be prepared every time you leave the house.

This should go without saying, because if you aren't 100 percent prepared when talking to a hiring manager or business contact, then quite frankly, you don't deserve to get the job. It's also important to expand this "preparedness" to situations in which you're talking to a newly-formed business contact who might not be a hiring manager per se, but is someone who's "plugged in" to an area in which you are interested.

Why? Because even though this person doesn't have a job for you right now, you never know who she may know who does have a job that fits your background.

Let's take a look at what it means to be prepared for these situations. First, you should carry business cards at all times. I've given you some thoughts on what those cards should look like

(Tip #7), and will show you how to best present them (Tip #10). Any way you look at it, having cards on you at all times is an absolute must.

Second, try to stay away from the "hard sell," even if it looks like this person can help you immediately. If the situation warrants, feel free to tell your story on how you can help other organizations address their challenges (remember, your contact doesn't have a job opening right now).

But if that doesn't seem appropriate, then exchange business cards and touch base with her in a few days to continue your discussion. Needless to say, following up is extremely important, especially in situations where the person has agreed to point you in the direction of another person who can help. By the way, this contact doesn't need to be someone you met at a traditional networking event. You could meet this person standing in line at the bank, waiting at the drive thru, or any other place you find yourself.

That's why being prepared is so important, because you never know who you're going to meet, or where it's going to happen. As a matter of fact, you won't even know if that person has a job to offer when you do meet them. All of that is out of your control. But you can control what you know and how you deliver that information. In addition, you also can tailor your message to include information that the other person would find of interest (Tip #4).

> ...make sure you have all your ducks in a row when it comes to presenting yourself to others, and see what happens to your confidence when other people start lending a hand.

So, if you have a good message with a good delivery, as well as some professional-looking business cards to back it up, then you're ready for any opportunity that presents itself. And truth

> ...as far as confidence is concerned, what a great way to feel better about yourself and the process by contributing to an organization you believe in.

be told, people are more inclined to help if they think you're already taking steps to help yourself. So make sure you have all your ducks in a row when it comes to presenting yourself to others, and see what happens to your confidence when other people start lending a hand.

Consider consulting (free of charge) with a small business in a related field as a way to keep your skills sharp.

Here's another thought that goes against conventional wisdom, but hear me out. Most small business owners have a lot of good ideas, but not a lot of time to implement them. Most job seekers, on the other hand, have a good bit of time on their hands, but not enough ideas on how to keep their professional skills sharp. So why not partner with a small business owner and see if he'd be willing to have you work, free of charge, for say 10 hours a week on a particular project of interest.

From the business owner's perspective, it's a definite win because he now has an additional resource working on a project that wasn't being addressed before. From your perspective, it's a great way to "get back in the game" and keep your skills sharp, while you're still networking and interviewing for a more permanent position.

And, as far as confidence is concerned, what a great way to feel better about yourself and the process by contributing to an organization you believe in. Remember in college when you or your friends interned with a corporation for little or no money to gain experience in a particular industry?

Well, this is the same thing, except this time it's better, because you get to choose where you work. And by the way, you also can use this project as a means of "filling in the gaps" on your resume, so it doesn't look as if you were out of work for such a long period of time. In my book, I'd call that a win-win situation.

"Can I Get Your Card?"

As a networking professional, those five words are music to your ears. Not only does it mark the end of the conversation, effectively freeing you up to meet other people at the event, but it also gives you the sign that this person wants to talk to you again.

But just as the 12 x 12 x 12 rule marks the beginning of people's first impression of you, the business card signifies the beginning of the next phase. (For an explanation of the 12 x 12 x 12 rule, please feel free to visit Our ToolBelt at www.agitoconsulting.com.)

Make no mistake about it, people are sizing you up from the moment they see you until the time you walk away, and you want to make sure you come out looking like a pro.

So with that in mind, let's take a look at a few of the basics when it comes to handing out and receiving business cards during a typical networking event.

Know where your cards are located.

I know this may sound a little funny, but I can't tell you how many times I've been winding down a good conversation with someone, asked them for their card

After mastering this technique, you'll look great, feel confident, and that'll be one more positive thing other people pick up on.

and then been given the wrong one.

Usually this person only uses one pocket to hold all of their cards, including the ones of people they've just met. So when they reach inside their pocket, the chances of picking out the wrong card are greatly increased.

Recommendation: Designate your left jacket pocket for new business cards you pick up, and your right one for your own.

After doing this a few times, you'll get into the habit of automatically reaching into your right pocket and taking out your card without interrupting your train of thought. After mastering this technique, you'll look great, feel confident, and that'll be one more positive thing other people pick up on.

Make a habit of writing notes on the back of other people's cards.

Let's assume for a minute that you attend two networking events a week and, generally speaking, you walk away with three to five cards from each event. Let's also say that on average it takes you about five minutes to have a conversation with someone, and ultimately create a rapport with that individual.

If you want to follow up with your new contacts a few days later and incorporate just a tidbit of your original conversation into that message, then that means you're going to have to keep track of a good 30 minutes worth of discussions with at least six different people, during a one-week time frame.
(3 cards x 5 minutes x 2 networking events per week.)

Sound like a lot of work? You bet.

But imagine yourself effortlessly incorporating your previous discussion into a follow-up email, without having to remember every single detail associated with that event. Sound too good to be true?

Actually, it's not. The next time you meet someone, try writing down some notes on the back of that person's card immediately after the conversation is over. That way you don't have to try to keep track of everything he just said.

Not sure what to write?

How about this: On the front of their card, write down the date and location of the event. Turn it over, and on the back, write down a couple of brief notes pertaining to the discussion you just had. It could be an area of professional interest this person has, or, if you're an entrepreneur, a potential area of business where the two of you can work together.

This also is a good time to write down any action steps you may have committed to during the conversation (sending an email, forwarding a phone number, etc). That way, when you follow up with an email a couple of days later, you'll be able to pick up right where you left off, and incorporate some of your original discussion into the email.

And believe me, when people see that, they'll know they're networking with a pro!

(For an example of what this email could look like, please visit our articles section on www.agitoconsulting.com.)

20

Accelerating your Success

Evaluate Your Networking Success

Here's the situation. It's 9:15 on a Wednesday night and you've just come home from your latest networking outing. You met a bunch of good contacts there, and even though you didn't meet any "big name" Fortune 500 executives, you walked away with five business cards of people you'd like to follow up with over the next few days.

Question: Was this a successful event? Well that depends on what you were hoping to get out of it. (For further discussion on this, see "Got Goals?" in Tip #16).

If you walked in there with the idea that you could "do some business" with people that night, as you "wheeled and dealed" your way towards closing a couple of sales, then no, your experience probably wasn't all that great. However, if you were expecting to come away with some new business contacts who might be able to help you now as well as further down the road, then yes, tonight can be classified as a wildly successful evening.

One of the biggest challenges facing networkers today is accurately determining the success of a particular event, and then using that information to decide if they should attend a similar event in the future. In other words, was this a good use of your time?

One of the biggest challenges facing networkers today is accurately determining the success of a particular event, and then using that information to decide if they should attend a similar event in the future.

While everyone can spot the "successful" event where they land a corporate account on the spot, the real question is, in the absence of a "home run," what factors should you use to evaluate your networking success?

Here are three questions I always ask myself on the drive home from a networking event.

Did you talk to enough people?

This might sound funny at first, since the objective of most networking events is to do just that, but, as I've found out over the years, some events are better than others when it comes to creating a solid networking environment.

As an example, I've attended a number of networking events that consisted of lunch or dinner functions where you sit down with 10 or 12 people at your table, after engaging in small talk with others on your way in. And while I've sometimes found the speakers at these events to be very helpful in terms of garnering new business (See Tip #5), I usually talk to the same two or three individuals sitting at my table.

For me, that's an example of an event where I didn't meet my objective.

Were the people you talked to in your target market?

Of course, before you can evaluate yourself in this area, you first have to determine who your target market is. And before you say "everyone," let me say that some customers are easier to get than others, so it pays to have an idea of who those people are.

As an example, let's say you're interested in finding female business owners with an average revenue of $30,000. If that's the case, then networking at business women's associations would probably be a much better place for you to start, than say your local chamber of commerce. Both options are good, but one is clearly a better draw for your clientele.

So after you figure out who your ideal customer is, you'll need to ask yourself where those people would be. After that, you can go online and find networking events that will most likely put you in contact with those individuals.

If you can't find ones that hit the spot exactly, then continue to network (you didn't think I was going to let you off the hook that easily did you), but do so with the idea of meeting new contacts who can point you in the direction of your prospective customers.

Did you secure business as a result of attending this event?

This question is actually trickier to answer than it might appear. When some people look at it, their first thought is whether they met a person at the event with whom they ultimately closed a deal. That's what I call "direct business closings" and this is something that's very important to measure. However, I'd like to expand that definition and ask, "Did you secure **any** business as a result of attending this event?"

In other words, did you meet someone who pointed you in the direction of someone else, who ultimately led you to another person who was in the market for what you had to sell?
(I told you it was a little tricky).

...in the absence of a "home run," what factors should you use to evaluate your networking success?

As an example, when I started my business a while back, one of the first places I started networking was with a popular service organization in the Atlanta area. I met with these folks every week for lunch, where we addressed club business and listened to a local speaker, who talked to us about his or her organization. Needless to say, when you see the same 20 or so people every week for lunch, you really get a chance to know them and their business.

So after awhile, word got out that I was a motivational speaker, and one day I got a call from our incoming president telling me the local chamber of commerce was looking for a speaker for their upcoming event, and would I be interested in filling in. To make a long story short, I spoke at the event and as a result met several people who have opened (and are continuing to open) doors for me much sooner than I ever could have done on my own.

While I haven't received any direct business from this service organization, I did get that speaking opportunity, which over time proved to be more valuable. So even if the event you attended didn't give you any direct business, the question you have to ask yourself is, "Did I meet other people who can have an impact on my career?" And by the way, the answer to that one isn't going to come overnight.

I'd recommend attending at least two or three sessions of the same event, following up with all the folks you met while you were there, and then making a determination as to how that impacted your business.

And yes, that's going to take time. But the last thing you want to do is to "cut bait" on a networking event because it didn't give you any new business the first time out.

When Can I Call This Person Back?

"Save early and often."

That's what a friend once said when it comes to creating computer files, because you just never know when the power is going to go out, taking everything you had with it.

And in the world of networking, I'd say similar advice holds true, especially when it comes to following up with someone you've just met. Because you never know when another company (for entrepreneurs) or another candidate (for job seekers) is going to surface and "steal" the contact you made the night before.

With that in mind, how long should you wait until you follow up with someone you just met? Personally, I recommend two days. That might sound odd at first, meeting someone Tuesday night then waiting until Thursday morning to call, but the last thing you want to do is appear overly anxious when contacting this person; especially if they're the decision maker (for entrepreneurs) or the hiring manager (for job seekers).

Remember, they have many other things going on as well. So by waiting a couple of days, you'll come across as the calm, cool professional who's staying on top of the situation, without being overly aggressive in the process.

Besides, if you're really interested in following up with someone, you'll need that time to get yourself ready for the next conversation.

Day One

The day after meeting your new contact, I'd recommend spending at least 35 to 40 minutes researching the company they represent. If you're a job seeker looking for an interview or an entrepreneur looking to close a sale, then a thorough visit to this company's Web site is an absolute must.

...by waiting a couple of days, you'll come across as the calm, cool professional who's staying on top of the situation, without being overly aggressive in the process.

You should research how the company has performed over the past two years, and how it's positioned for next year. You should also look up the names of the top executives, and search the Web to see if any articles were published about them over the past 12 months.

"Drill down" as much as possible, focusing on a particular division or area within the company (preferably the one that syncs up with the area in which your contact is located), and then jot down a few questions specific to that area.

After that, I'd recommend calling the company's main number (obtained from the Web site) and ask to speak with someone in public relations who might be able to answer some of the questions you wrote down. If the company you're calling is relatively small, and you don't want to risk your contact knowing you called beforehand, consider having a trusted friend contact the company and ask some of your questions. That way you don't have to worry about appearing overly aggressive.

Once you've got all of that, I'd recommend spending an additional 15 minutes (which puts us at a total of about one hour) generating questions as it relates to your specific objective. (For some ideas on the "right" questions to ask, please see Tip #15.)

Day Two

Now it's time to make "the call." Personally, I like to make these early in the day, say between eight and nine o'clock in the morning, when most people are usually at their desks.

You should have your list of questions (and key points) at the ready, as well as a blank sheet of paper to jot down any notes.

As a final word of advice, I like to call people twice before leaving a voicemail. With so many voicemails being left on everyone's machines, I've found it more efficient to not leave one the first time around, in the hopes that you can catch them an hour or so later. If you don't reach your contact after two tries, then make sure you leave a "benefit driven message" (see Tip #17) and make a note to follow up with them a week from today.

That way if the person is out of town, or if they're just swamped, you don't come across as being overly aggressive by calling every two days.

And there you have it, a quick and easy blueprint on how long you should wait, and what to do while you're waiting, for every person you meet.

How to Talk So Others Will Listen

You've just returned from your networking event, and boy did you nail it! Not only did you run into a few people you knew and spent time reestablishing those relationships, but a colleague introduced you to one of the local "big wigs" in town.

And if that wasn't good enough, it looks like his company is thinking about contracting out some of the very same services your small business can provide. You didn't get into all the details, but he did give you his card and asked that you call him later in the week.

Wow!

Now, we know you're not going to call right away, because he needs a couple of days to get back in the office and get himself situated. (Apparently he's been out of town for the past week.) But that's okay because I just gave you some ideas on what you should do to prepare yourself for that next interaction (Tip #12).

Fast-forward a couple of days to 8:20 a.m., when it's time to make "the call." Sure, you're a little nervous, but the real question is: How can you persuade him to outsource the work to your company? In other words, what can you do to get his business?

How can you persuade him to outsource the work to your company? In other words, what can you do to get his business?

That's actually an easy one. Use an Agito Consulting "Benefit Statement" to drive your discussion.

But first, some background.

Before we get into the details of exactly how you do that, let's take a step back and look at two other statements, factual and feature, that can help us better understand where we're trying to go.

A factual statement, as the name implies, is one where a truth or actuality is clearly stated. As an example I could say, "Agito Consulting is a motivational speaking corporation." It's short, sweet and to the point.

The feature statement is also factually based, but it contains specific attributes, or characteristics related to that particular subject. In this example, I could say, "Our company specializes in three other areas within the motivational speaking field— leadership skills, customer service and effective communication."

Feature statements are mostly seen in marketing and sales-related materials, and generally speaking, do a decent job of conveying a message. However, with feature statements, you always run into one little catch: They consist of the specific attributes and qualities that the speaker deems important, regardless of their relevance to the listener. In other words, a feature statement talks about the bells and whistles of a particular product, without showing how those bells and whistles can help the listener.

Example:
"Our car is the fastest automobile in its class." What if safety is my #1 concern?

"Our computer has the lowest price of every other system in the industry." What if money isn't my primary buying factor?

The point is that in both of these situations, the salesman uses feature statements about the products—the speed of the car and the price of the computer—but doesn't address what may be important to the buyer. Unless those features are important to me, that's not going to influence my purchasing decision.

An Alternative: The "Benefit Statement"

Fortunately, we have an answer to this quandary: The Agito Consulting "Benefit Statement." This is exactly like the feature statement, except it contains specific attributes or qualities relevant to the listener. If you want to influence a person's decision, then you need to give them the specific benefits associated with taking your desired course of action.

As an example, let's say I'm talking to an executive who tells me he can't stand all of the sniping among his employees. He feels the people on his staff are constantly stabbing each other in the back, and he just doesn't see why they can't work together as a team.

He doesn't mind a little friendly competition among professionals, but the situation has gone beyond that, and it's starting to cost the company money. After asking a few more questions along those lines, and listening to his responses, I finally give him the following statement:

"Our workshop helps diffuse conflict by resolving interpersonal challenges with specific techniques for dealing with everyone around you. Is this something you'd like to learn more about?"

> If you want to influence a person's decision, then you need to give them the specific benefits associated with taking your desired course of action.

Wow!

Now that's a statement. If you were him, wouldn't you want to at least hear what I had to say regarding a problem that you've already voiced? Of course you would.

Making The Call

Getting back to the original situation where you're getting ready to call the local "big wig", how can you create a "benefit statement" that's sure to knock his socks off?

For starters, you could ask what got his company started in this direction in the first place. In other words, based on your initial conversation, your service was something they were considering contracting out even before you met. So what got them headed in that direction?

Was it declining sales, increased competition, new regulatory factors? Something made them want to do this, and you need to find out what that is. Once you know that information, you can turn it around and create a "benefit statement" that works for your situation.

As an example, let's say during your follow-up phone call you casually ask what got the company started in this direction, and he replies that the competition is eating them alive because they provide a service his company doesn't offer.

After asking a few more questions, you can give him a "benefit statement" that sounds like this:

"Our company specializes in product rollout and design, and as a matter of fact, our turnaround time is one of the lowest in the industry. We can develop your product, and roll it out in a fraction of the time you might be used to. Is that something you'd like to learn more about?"

Bang!

See how you were able to hit his main challenge—time in this case—and turn it into a benefit your company offers?

If you'd like an example of another question you can ask to help bring out the key challenge in your prospective customer's mind, please refer to Tip #15, "Three (More) Easy Questions to Stand Out from the Crowd".

But for now, pick up the phone and make that call!

Create Your Very Own Networking Database

With all this talk about securing quality business contacts through effective networking techniques, I'd be remiss if I didn't recommend a few options for organizing these names.

Now when it comes to creating a networking database, you have almost as many options as there are people using them. But for today, we'll focus on the main three that I've seen, and then you can find the one that works best for you.

The "Shoebox" Method.

This is one of the most basic methods, and it's probably one we've all used at one time or another. As the name implies, it involves taking a box to store all of your newly obtained business cards. Then, you can put that box on your desk, or someplace close to it, and you'll have all of your cards in one place.

Why you should consider using this system:
- Easy to implement.
- Takes very little time to maintain.
- Good "first step" if you're just starting out.

Why this might not work for you:
- Very time consuming to find one particular person's name.
- This system becomes harder to use as you meet more people and get more cards.

Comments: Unless your cards are all over the place, you can probably find another system that better suits your needs.

Use a business card organizer.

Most professionals implement some variant of this method; they either use a Rolodex®, or a business card folder. However, just because everyone else is using it, don't feel like you need to follow the crowd.

Why you should consider using this system:
- Very easy to maintain once it's started.
- Highly portable and easy to take a person's name with you on the road.
- Convenient for other people to access your network even when you're out of the office.

Why this might not work for you:
- All of your eggs are truly in one basket. If something should happen to your Rolodex®, or if you should lose your business card folder, then you've wiped out your entire networking base.
- Easy for cards to get lost in the shuffle, especially if you travel frequently and if people constantly are looking through your Rolodex®.

Comments: This method can definitely work for just about anybody, from a new person breaking into the ranks, or a seasoned pro who's "been around the block."

E-Nabling your network.

With all the contact management software around, this method actually is a lot easier to implement today than it was 10 years ago. As an example, I've seen an Excel™, spreadsheet, or even an Access™, database, used as a way of capturing contact information. (I've also seen Word™, used in a similar fashion, but that's not really the answer because it gets very unwieldy as the network grows.)

If you're feeling particularly aggressive, take a look at what Act!® or some other contact management companies offer, and see if that works for you. I go into more detail on this option in Tip #20, but it really depends on your budget and what you hope to accomplish with the system.

Why you should consider using this system:
- Very easy to find people once you have got the database up and running.
- Relatively easy for someone else to find a contact's phone number when you're out of the office.
- Your entire network can be "backed up" electronically.

Why this might not work for you:
- Somewhat time-consuming to set up (especially if you're migrating from the shoebox method).
- Requires you to spend a little more time to input people's names after each networking event. (Instead of just slipping cards into your Rolodex®, you have to input the data into the system.)

Comments: Personally, I like this method best due to the added benefit of backing up the data. You never know what's going to happen on any given day, and for me, the peace of mind that comes from having another copy of my network database is priceless.

Another reason E-Nabling works for me is that now I have the option of capturing information that goes beyond the traditional approach. Each time I meet someone, I input their name, phone number, company name, how I met them (if referred by a mutual friend), and where my prospective clients are in the sales cycle. Again, for the way I like to operate, this added flexibility is absolutely perfect.

Now take a look at each option, figure out which one you like best, and make sure to implement it right away!

Three (More) Easy Questions to Stand Out from the Crowd

Earlier in the book we talked about the importance of standing out in people's minds, through the "What About Me?" technique (Tip #4).

Now that the event is over, and you've walked away with a few business cards, the next question becomes, "What next?" In other words, how are you going to build upon the rapport you've already created?

Answer: By doing exactly what you did when you first met.

Combine good listening skills with solid questions, and continue to add value to the conversation. This time however, it's going to be better, because you've had a couple of days to think about it, and the questions will specifically relate to this particular person.

Let's take a look at some examples from two different perspectives: One as an entrepreneur who met a potential client, and the other as a person who's looking for an employment opportunity.

"So let me ask you something, as the [Senior Vice President] of [Your Company], what's the one thing that keeps you up at night?"

A colleague brought this question to my attention, and I recommend it for any entrepreneur looking to win the next deal. I like it because it allows you to identify the specific challenge(s) this person is currently facing, and presumably, if you position your product or service in the context of addressing that challenge, then you've won yourself a customer.

Needless to say, this shouldn't be the first question right out of the gate when you're following up with someone. During most phone calls, you'll have time for a little small talk and then a few questions. I recommend this be the last one on the list.

One more thing, if it turns out that your prospective customer surprises you by answering the question in a way that precludes your business from helping him out, that's fine. At least you found out early in the process, and you can ask about contacting him a few months down the road.

Just because they're not facing a challenge that you can address today doesn't mean they won't have something come up later.

In another scenario, what if a prospective client asks you about price during a follow-up call, how should you respond? Here's an example.

"Generally speaking, our services range from two to four hour sessions, and we're looking at a range of $X to $Y depending on the length of the workshop. Is that in line with what you expected?"

Pay special attention to that last part, because that's what creates a win-win situation for you.

If the price isn't what he expected, then you'll find out what the prospective client had in mind, and the two of you may still work something out. Conversely, if that range was along the lines of what he expected, then you don't have to worry about any big surprises later because price has already been quantified. Either way, you come out looking like a pro.

Now let's say you're a job seeker who met someone who wasn't a hiring manager himself, but who knows of someone else in your industry who is. How do you get that person's contact information when you're following up with the original contact you met? How about this:

"During our last conversation, we talked about some of the experience I had in the computer industry, and how you thought that [contact name] would be a good person for me to meet. What made you think of her regarding my expertise?"

This question accomplishes two things: First, it's a memory jogger for your original contact, allowing him to recall your conversation without asking you what it was in regard to. Second, it allows you to get the hiring manager's contact information, while still coming across as a cool, confidant professional.

And remember, networking is less about meeting new people than it is having them remember you after the fact. So just stick with these questions, while developing some of your own, and you'll be well on your way to increased personal success.

TIP
16

Got Goals?

Fact: In Atlanta, you can attend between seven and twelve networking events on any given weekday.

And considering each event will likely run at least an hour, it's easy to see how there just isn't enough time in the day to do it all. So how do you decide which events to attend and which ones to "pass" on? Create an overall objective as to who you want to meet, and then develop a set of goals to correspond with that mission.

To start out, I'd recommend looking at your existing customers and think back to where you met them. How exactly did it happen? Was it through a friend, a referral, or a networking event? Assuming you met some of them at networking events, which ones were they, and have you attended them again? (If they worked once in getting you a new client, then chances are they could work again.)

Goal #1: Attend 90 percent of the [Successful Networking Event's] meetings over the next 90 days.

Okay, now that we've got that established, are there any other events similar to the ones you've already identified as being successful? As an example, if you've found your local chamber of commerce to be particularly successful in finding new clients, then perhaps you should start attending meetings in surrounding chamber locations. For those of you in the Atlanta area, there are at least three within a 40-minute drive of each other.

Goal #2: Attend one new networking event each month.

Now that we've got the first two goals, here's our situation: You're attending events that have been successful in the past, and you've made it a priority to attend a new meeting at least once a month. But what about the actual events themselves? Should you "drill down" a bit and attach specific goals to those individual sessions?

Absolutely. As a matter of fact, here are a couple of addit-ional goals I'd recommend using every time you go to an event.

Goal #3: Meet three to five new business contacts at every networking event.

Some people might think getting three to five new contacts per session is woefully inadequate, and instead say they want to "work the room" by getting as many business cards as possible.

While that may work for them, remember that networking is less about meeting new people than it is having them remember you after the fact. If you're running from person to person, stopping for two minutes and dropping off your business card before moving on to the next person, how are you going to find the time to add value to that conversation, and subsequently stand out from the crowd?

Personally, I like to spend about five to seven minutes listening and talking to people (in that order), so I can understand where they're coming from. That way, I can have something of sub-stance to say later when I'm following up on that discussion.

Goal #4: Follow up with each new business contact via phone or email, within 48 hours of meeting them.

Now some people might balk at that because they don't see the value in doing it, don't think they have the time, or don't know what to say. In terms of the value, that comes from the fact that no one else is doing it.

Ninety five percent of the new people I meet at networking events never take the time to follow up with a quick "nice talking to you" email, even though it only takes 5 minutes to write. Sending an email to someone (even though they're not a prospective client) is a great way, in and of itself, to stand out from the crowd.

The next issue is what to say. Let's take a look at an email I've used.

"John, my name is Brian Hilliard and I'm a motivational speaker who met you at the chamber of commerce meeting last week. During our discussion we talked about how much the chamber has changed over the past few years, and if Thursday's speakers were any indication, I can't wait to see what the next 5 years will bring!
Again, it was great talking to you, and if I can help you out in any way, please let me know."

I got the last part from a friend of mine, Mike Litman, author of the book **Conversations With Millionaires,** because I think it adds a nice touch to the whole process. But as you can see, I didn't really have to say too much; just a quick note saying I appreciated our time together, and if I can be of service in the future to please let me know. If you received an email like that, would you be more inclined to remember that person two months down the line?

You bet.

Get Your Voicemails Returned Right Away

Earlier in the book we talked about how the "benefit statement" can make you a more influential person with everyone you meet (Tip #13). While that's still the case in your regular day-to-day interactions, there's another aspect to the "benefit statement" that can help get your voicemails returned right away!

I like to call the process of integrating a "benefit statement" into a voicemail a "Benefit Driven Message," and it has two advantages over a conventional voicemail message. First, it increases the odds that your message will be returned in a timely fashion, and as any businessperson knows, that alone is good enough to give it a try. Second, the "benefit driven message" makes the recipient more receptive to what you have to say.

Why is that? Because your message quickly and easily answers the most basic question that almost everyone in the business world wants to know: What's in it for me?

Let's take a look at some examples of a benefit driven message, and how it can help you get your calls returned right away.

Job Seeker

"Bob, my name is Brian Hilliard, and we met at the chamber event a few days ago. During our discussion we talked about the computer industry, and how the oversupply has adversely impacted pricing across the country.

I found an article that looks at it from a different angle, and I'm emailing it to you now. And as a matter of fact, I have a few ideas on how I think your business can benefit from the situation.

If you could give me a call at (404) 434-2826, I'd appreciate it."

In this example we're assuming you created a contact—not necessarily a hiring manager, but someone who might be able to help—and now you're following up with that individual. And since we know most individuals are reluctant to speak with someone who's just "looking for a job," we've left a message containing value for the other person.

In this case, some additional information about the computer industry and some thoughts on how he can best use it to help his company. (After he calls you back).

When I teach this concept in workshops, one frequent question is, "What do I do if I don't have an article that's relevant to our discussion?"

Answer: You need to find one.

Even if it's not 100 percent on track in terms of the exact discussion you had, you need to find something that's relatively close. Remember, as a job seeker, most business people automatically assume that when you call them you're going to ask for a job. And, if they don't have a job to give you right now, what do you think the chances are of them calling you back? Probably not too good.

But, if you have some information that can help them, then

you've created a differentiating factor between yourself and everyone else. Sure it will take some work, but use the "advanced functions" on the Google™ search engine, and you should have no problem finding what you need.

Just make sure you're using the "email this article to a friend" option, so you won't violate any copyright laws in the process.

(My lawyer made me put that in).

Entrepreneur

"Joan, my name is Brian Hilliard, and we met at the chamber event a few days ago. I was looking at your Web site yesterday, and noticed the high level of involvement your company has in the local community.

As a matter of fact, I recently worked with a company that implemented a similar strategy. We hosted a blood drive with the local Red Cross, and while we haven't received the official numbers, based on my observations, it was a real winner.

I've seen some other ideas work as well, if you'd like to give me a call at (404) 434-2826. Thanks."

In this situation you can see how you can clearly differentiate yourself from the competition by providing an idea that your potential client can use right away, in this case, partnering with the local Red Cross for a blood drive.

Even if that's something they've done before, you've at least demonstrated a willingness to think about the situation from the other person's perspective. If your potential client doesn't have a Web site, then you'll have to rely on your notes from the original conversation, as well as your general industry experience to create a compelling reason for this person to call you back. (See why it's important to read everyday?)

Oh, and by the way, it's going to take you a good 15 to 20

minutes to come up with a solid "benefit driven message"—one where the listener stops what they're doing and takes notice. But take my word for it, it's time well spent. Not only do you increase the chances of her calling you back, you also get yourself noticed. So if you have to follow up again, say via email this time, you're more likely to show up on her radar screen.

Conclusion

Needless to say, with all this talk about voicemails and getting people to call you back, you'll want to keep a few basics in mind when leaving a message:

- Keep your message under 30 seconds.

- Know what you want to say, and write your message down before you pick up the phone. (I know that sounds like a lot, but believe me, it'll sound a lot smoother.)

- Always leave your phone number, and make sure you say it slowly at the end of the call. (Remember, the other person is trying to write it down.)

- Give your message the old "once over," preferably out loud, prior to delivering.

There you have it. The "secret sauce" if you will, of getting your voicemails returned right away!

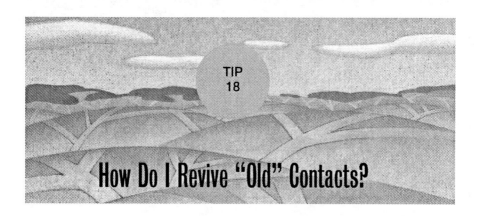

How Do I Revive "Old" Contacts?

Generally speaking, I recommend that individuals touch base with newly formed business contacts within 48 hours of their initial meeting, and a good bit of what you've read so far is designed to help you achieve that goal. However, with many of the people I see in our workshops, one question remains constant: "What about all of the other contacts I made before coming here? How can I reconnect with those people, many of whom I haven't talked to in quite some time?"

Great question.

First, no one is ever going to stay in touch with everyone they meet at every networking event. There are just too many people, and not enough time in the day. And just as different people ebb and flow out of your personal network, much the same can happen in the business world.

But for the sake of discussion, let's assume we're talking about people you've met within the last six to twelve months, and for whatever reason, you've fallen out of touch. How can you reconnect with them? Well here are three of my personal favorites that I use whenever it's time to revive "old" contacts.

Send a postcard.

This is one you can use just about any time, but it's especially good when you're heading out of town.

Whenever I get away for a few days, I usually pick out 9 or 10 people that I haven't spoken to in a while, and make it a point to drop them a line.

I write down their addresses before I leave, and bring plenty of stamps so I can mail them off before I set foot back in my house. Because we all know what it's like coming back from a trip: You have 20 voicemails and 50 emails, and it will take you week to dig out from under that pile. But, by having all of my "material" with me while I'm away, I can make sure they're sent out in a timely fashion.

And by the way, in terms of the actual message, it doesn't have to be anything too fancy, just a quick note to touch base and refresh the relationship. As an example, I might write something like this:

"Hello from sunny North Carolina! I managed to get out of the office for a few days and I just wanted to touch base to see how things were going. I know I've been super busy myself, but maybe we can get together sometime for coffee or a bite to eat. It'd be great to catch up! In the meantime though, have yourself a great week and I look forward to keeping in touch."

If your next trip is a little ways off, consider using a digital camera to create postcards you can send right away. I sometimes use pictures I've taken from previous vacations, print them off on nice paper and out they go. In either case, postcards are a great way to reestablish yourself in the mind of the other person, and can pave the way for a follow-up phone call or email down the road.

Send "value add" articles.

One of the benefits I mentioned in "Top 5 Reasons Why You Should Read Every Day" (Tip #6) was leveraging the vast amount of information, by highlighting an article you think someone else might value. Remember, this is a person you haven't spoken to in a while, so you need to be fairly certain that what you're sending them is on target. But, what better way to reconnect than by forwarding an article of interest? And by the way, the article doesn't always have to be entirely business-related either.

As an example, I recently sent an article to a personal contact of mine who is very much into golf. It was a feature on the No. 1 player on tour, and I thought he would get some enjoyment out of it. Nothing business-related there, but it did provide an opportunity to stay in touch.

A number of Web sites have an "email this article to a friend" option that allows you to quickly and easily send it off to an interested third party.

Send Holiday cards.

Of the three options listed in this chapter, I'd consider this one to be my least favorite. Not because sending holiday cards is bad, but because during the holidays, everyone is doing the exact same thing, so it's tough to stand out from the crowd.

But, if you haven't talked to this person in a while, and they didn't make the list for our first two options, then this is a good "stand-by" to at least get yourself back on the radar screen.

My recommendation is to send out your cards right after Thanksgiving, that way they can be among the first to arrive in your contact's mailbox.

My recommendation is to send out your cards right after Thanksgiving, that way they can be among the first to arrive in your contact's mailbox. Personally, I have our cards out by December 1st, so people get them before being bombarded by other holiday well-wishers.

So when it comes to creating a new business relationship, I strongly recommend you follow-up with that person within the first couple of days. But, if that's not possible, here are three easy ways to help you reconnect.

Develop an Inner Circle of Networking Professionals

Throughout this book we've addressed a number of different networking techniques that can help you meet new people, and have other people want to meet you.

You've learned how to stand out from the crowd (Tip #3) and how to get your card to the top of the stack (Tip #7). You've become more persuasive with everyone you meet (Tip #4) and you've developed goals to get you where you need to go (Tip #16). In short, you're networking like a pro!

But if you want to take yourself to the next level, then developing a close group of business contacts is a great first step. I refer to these contacts as your "inner circle," and as a networking professional myself, I've found this to be one of the most difficult skills to master.

Why? Because developing those relationships requires commitment from both individuals. And in our fast food, drive thru, "Do you want fries with that?" culture, most people don't have the patience required to create such close business contacts.

Instead, they would rather meet five new people at their next networking event, hoping that one or two might be good contacts, instead of having coffee with someone they already know and deepening that relationship. Because when you think about it, the people you know the best probably know you pretty well too. And if that's the case, why not continue to develop that mutually beneficial relationship?

Still not convinced? Here are my top three reasons why I recommend developing an "inner circle."

They can provide referrals.

As most entrepreneurs or business people will attest to, referrals are the lifeblood of any successful enterprise. Outside of the customers you work with every day, who better to give you a referral than a close professional contact that knows your business and is comfortable with the service you provide?

> Personally, when it comes to referrals, I only give them to people I've come to know over a series of phone calls, emails, and maybe even coffee.

Personally, when it comes to referrals, I only give them to people I've come to know over a series of phone calls, emails, and maybe even coffee. I don't want to risk putting my name on the line by referring someone to another person I don't know very well.

As an example, I have an inner circle friend of mine to whom I've referred clients for more than a year, and we enjoy talking shop every once in a while over a bite to eat. Little did I know that prior to us getting together one day, she'd been thinking about me for a potential speaking opportunity, and our lunch provided the perfect outlet for that referral to be passed along.

Boy was I surprised! And to think that it could have just as easily gone the other way if neither of us had made it a priority to get together that afternoon.

You can bounce ideas off of them.

Let's face it, no matter how smart or how sharp you and your team might be, it's never a bad idea to bounce some ideas off of a third party. Whether you're an entrepreneur looking for the next Big Idea, or a job seeker looking for a new direction, having that "extra" person around can do wonders for your professional success.

I was fortunate to run into Amy Windham, a sales and marketing professional, a few months ago, and I can't tell you how instrumental she's been in filling this role. As a business owner, it's easy to get carried away with the latest idea or gadget, and for me, Amy has been someone who always seems to have my best interests in mind.

If you don't have someone in your business world who's filling that role for you, I'd recommend taking a closer look at your existing contact list and see if someone catches your eye. You're obviously not going to call them up and ask, "Would you like you to join my inner circle?" But, you can call them and ask if they'd like to have lunch in the next couple of weeks. Be sure to let them know beforehand that you'd like to bounce some business ideas off of them, and see what they say.

> If you don't have someone in your business world who's filling that role for you, I'd recommend taking a closer look at your existing contact list and see if someone catches your eye.

Now if you don't find anyone on your list who jumps out at you, that's fine too. Just make finding a person like that a priority, and keep it in mind as you're talking to new people at networking events.

They can provide you with a NetWeaving™ opportunity.

If you haven't heard this term before, a friend of mine, Bob Littell, introduced this concept in his book **The Heart and Art of NetWeaving: Building Meaningful Relationships One Connection at a Time.** NetWeaving™ is a system that shows individuals how they can play a pivotal role in other people's lives, by connecting them to other people they know who can help them out.

As an example, Bob took it upon himself to introduce me to someone in his network. He introduced us, we all went out to lunch, and bang! Now, I know one of Bob's contacts, and he has proven to be very helpful to my business.

This is an especially powerful technique for all parties involved, and if you haven't seen it in action, I'd recommend picking up a copy of his book.

In the context of developing an inner circle, NetWeaving™ is the perfect answer. Who else would you feel more comfortable with in setting up a NetWeaving™ opportunity than someone you know really well? And believe me, when you give this technique a try, the reward you'll get will be greater than what you could have imagined. Doors you hadn't even dreamed existed will begin to open.

So before you head out to your next networking event, consider giving an "old" contact a call and getting together for coffee or lunch. Because you just never know when deepening an existing relationship is actually better than creating a new one.

Save Time with Technology

All right, now you've reached the final tip in the book. You've created solid networking goals, and you're evaluating your success every time you come back from an event. You've engaged keynote speakers during their presentations, and you're standing out by asking the right questions.

In short, you're networking like a pro.

But how can a networking professional such as yourself keep up with all these new people? After all, it's easy to remember the details when you only have a few contacts, but as your network begins to grow, it's only a matter of time until someone "slips through the cracks."

So let's take a look at some technological products that will help you to continue to meet new people, without drowning yourself in the process.

Purchase some type of "contact management" software.

One of the best things I did for my business was to purchase software that allowed me to better manage my networking contacts. Not only did it help me keep track of a larger number of people, but it also reduced the stress associated with a growing list, because I stopped worrying that I'd forget to follow up with any one person.

That's right, I'm recommending going out to your local retail outlet, and picking up one of those small audio recorders that can go just about anywhere you do.

All I had to do was put their name in my software system, copy the notes I wrote on the back of their business card, and then set the "primer" for when I wanted to talk to them again. This helped remind me to make phone calls, send emails, and even contact people who were in my "inner circle" (Tip #19). Not to mention it also allowed other people in my office to easily access my schedule, and know where I am at any point in time.

From a pricing standpoint, you're looking at a $200 investment for one of the leading products in contact management software. If that sounds a little steep, I've also seen people use Microsoft Outlook™ as a contact management tool, since it contains many of the features (calendar, reminder settings, etc.) the other software has.

And depending on when you purchased your computer, Microsoft Outlook™ is probably already installed on your system. So take a look around, see what works best for you and then pull the trigger on something you like.

Consider purchasing a Personal Digital Assistant (PDA).

PDA's are a great way to keep up with all of your contacts, especially if you're on the road a lot or otherwise out of the office. It allows you to keep track of your calendar and your "to do" list, as well as capture contact information of people you just met.

And if that wasn't enough, on some of the latest systems you can actually transfer data from one machine to the next. So if you meet someone who has a compatible PDA and you want to get contact information for someone they know, you can electronically transfer that information from one PDA to the other.

When it comes to pricing, it really does depend on how you're planning to use it. If you're just looking for a basic address book, calendar and "to do" list, then you can get by with something under a $100. But if you're looking for state-of-the-art equipment, then a $600 purchase isn't out of the question. Figure out what functions are most valuable to you, and find one that fits your budget.

Buy a portable audio recorder.

With all this talk of technological products, I thought I'd end on one that's been around (it seems) since the beginning of time: The good old-fashioned tape recorder.

That's right, I'm recommending going out to your local retail outlet, and picking up one of those small audio recorders that can go just about anywhere you do.

Personally, I seem to have my best thoughts at some of the most inopportune times—like when I'm driving, or waiting at the dentist's office. Whenever that happens, I spend so much time scrambling for a piece of paper (while also trying to keep the car on the road), that by the time I'm ready to write, I've already lost my train of thought. But now that I have a portable cassette recorder, all I do is take it out of my pocket, note the time and date, and start talking. Then the next morning, I take out a fresh sheet of paper and jot down all the ideas I had from the previous day.

In terms of pricing, I was able to pick up mine for $50, but I'm sure that number varies depending on where you go and when you buy it.

If that sounds a little too much, another variant is to leave yourself a voicemail whenever you get a good idea. So instead of capturing it on a cassette recorder, you're doing it on your voicemail system. Same concept, just a different technique. There you have it, three small, relatively inexpensive technological products that can make your life a lot easier while you're networking like a pro.

NOTES

NOTES

NOTES

NOTES